PROPELLER BOOKS CONTEMPORARY POETRY SERIES

EDITORS   *Lucas Bernhardt and Jan Verberkmoes*

ELIZABETH/THE STORY OF DRONE

LOUISE AKERS

PROPELLER BOOKS

PORTLAND, OREGON • UNITED STATES OF AMERICA

First U.S. Edition, 2022

For further information, contact Propeller Books,
4325 Northeast Davis Street, Portland, OR 97213.

Cover photo by Lukasz Lada
Cover and interior design by Context

Published by Propeller Books, Portland, Oregon
ISBN 978-1-95559-302-1

www.propellerbooks.com

CONTENTS

ELIZABETH/THE STORY OF DRONE

a millennial apodictic

"Each of us is the mystagogue and the spotter of another."
—Jacques Derrida

MUSEUM

this is the story of drone.

it begins without becoming,
more like the entering and/or re-entering of a decisive structure,
oblique orientation. no futurity.

no orientation? no futurity. no processor.
limit: antecedent.
limit: no future. no decisive

orientation.
no structure.

no, no form.

how was it
at the museum?

i remember yellow drapes back from the cleaners, the single client
in the doorway.

what about it did you love.
what did you love about it the most?

i loved the monitors that loved each other. they spoke to each
other all day in their television language.

i loved them the most.

elizabeth wanted to die. wanted badly to live in our collective
imagination as a ghost

at once,
and oriented toward:

the glossy, level table,
the table full of ghosts/ghostdata.

elizabeth said: don't you remember what happens to carbon like
us?

this is the story of drone.
it begins in the asteroid belt.
god gradually migrated to earth, a relocation that made him more
logical and comprehensible. to know him became inadvertent,
continuous. people grew up around his knowledge, and in a
generation he was integrated into the human genome.

we lookedup. we began to lookup and feel
belonging, because of our new human organization,

genetically.

how were we organized before? is also a question of orientation.
it begins with a vertical leap.

we learned how little we could see, looking down. i mean how
much, but indistinct. tiny.
(oh, limit.)

anomaly became the singular referent, the utilitarian qualifier
par excellence: watch for change. recognize shape, memorize
behavioral patterns. no appreciable deviance may avoid
consequence/does not warrant an impactful and direct response.

orientation suggests futurity.
if you are a drone, your orientation is vertical, i.e., down=futurity.
if you are a drone pilot, your orientation is horizontal, toward a
monitor in the u.s. american west
(winter of.)

/(failure to.)

it begins with motor function. exported human organization, new
organization. external good.
sense in the wake of.

it begins in catalyst season.

it begins with lookingup again and again and thinking, how long
could something live up there when he,
well, he's down here!?
it starts with the difficulty of finding the stairs.

it begins with the following transcript:

SENSOR OPERATOR: They're praying, they're praying. . . .
This is definitely it, this is their force. Praying? I mean
seriously, that's what they do.
MISSION INTELLIGENCE COORDINATOR: They're gonna do
something nefarious.
. . .
01:50
MISSION INTELLIGENCE COORDINATOR: Adolescent near the
rear of the SUV.
SENSOR OPERATOR: Well, teenagers can fight.
MISSION INTELLIGENCE COORDINATOR: Pick up a weapon
and you're a combatant, it's how that works.
. . .
01:52
SENSOR OPERATOR: One guy still praying at the front of
the truck.
PILOT: JAG25 KIRK97 be advised, all pax [passengers] are
finishing up praying and rallying up near all three vehicles
at this time.
SENSOR OPERATOR: Oh, sweet target. I'd try to go through
the bed, put it right dead center of the bed.
MISSION INTELLIGENCE COORDINATOR: Oh, that'd be
perfect.
. . .
02:41
SENSOR OPERATOR: Well, sir, would you mind if I took a
bathroom break real quick?
PILOT: No, not at all, dude.
. . .
03:17
UNKNOWN: What's the master plan, fellas?
PILOT: I don't know, hope we get to shoot the truck with
all the dudes in it.
SENSOR OPERATOR: Yeah.

8

elizabeth said something about dying tomorrow or later,
something different about the next day.

god on earth changed our human organization, shifting human fear which is the large part of that organization.
fear became oriented. up toward him and then over toward each other. then up again, toward each other.

anomaly became the quintessential datasource: ghostdata. tables evolved into monitors—sophisticated measures were taken.
it begins with the literal ghosts in the machines.

an orientation of fear suggests futurity, reflects the unbroken potential for violence. the present lookup—everyone becomes a spotter.
the futurity of violence suggests it may pass, even if the likelihood is that it may occur. the orientation of fear determines the exact contours of the possibility of hope.

it begins: in some places, some people started therapy.

it begins with tidings of insurrection and its inchoate suppression. in the asteroid belt. in the u.s. america. winter of.

it follows human re-organization and the re-orientation of fear that the technologies
of delivering violence have changed.

this is the present lookup—know it?

10

1910: an act of state violence is reported by dictation, transcribed into writing, configured into telegraphic code, transmitted over copper wire, received, decrypted, transcribed by hand (in pencil) onto a telegraphic form, copied longhand, and verified by a functionary who signs his own name.

today, the pressures of restraint are vertical. the forces guiding us toward caricature, toward alienation funnel straight down.

elizabeth calls what we're doing monstrous and/or
phenomenology. she says it just like that, "phenomenology."

drone orientation is vertical=heterosexual.
ask what is the relationship between our contemporary means of
distributing death, and the aesthetic forms by which that death is
transmitted, recoded, mediated?

ask why some things are written in the passive voice.

say "oh my god" in the passive voice.

it begins with the disambiguation of the word 'vector,'

with the marxist understanding of time as a vector; the
inauguration of the present in recorded time; the disassembling of
progenitors; the disassembling of futurity along with antecedent.

god is the antecedent of drones. easy.

elizabeth said: if you exercise some patience, i will get to my point.

it begins with the possibility of the presence of oxygen on other
planets, detected
in the freeze/
the frozen surface
gunk. it begins with waking up and getting up and out
of the ocean everyday
for work.

it begins with ocean and the slender freeze of surface.

it begins with lumber, really. orientated down then hoisted back
up. conical.
in defense of,
(autumn of).

what was your favorite part of the museum?

the televisions that loved each other. the monitors that advertised
the reciprocity
of attack.

i loved the big, fat walls and the way the visitors examined them.

the thick doors with ankles for latches. time moving through
them diversely,
obliquely.

elizabeth thinks: it's my narcissism
silvering. the autumn of? or
winter of/ already/

failure to.

it begins in the asteroid belt with metal. early metal. the progenitors of metal and the metal antecedents.

the futurity of metal?

the lookup.

if one monitor went out, we would turn them all off, and wait.
that was essentially our way of telling them we loved them, too.
we appreciated how old they were and tired after all their years
and cities. we would take care of them now. let them rest as
needed, preserve their individual and convex dignities.

it begins with one. the single monitor with the cable, bolt and
socket, with the switch, the surge protector's 'off'/ 'on'.

i am standing in the center of the monitors, alone,
waiting.

it begins with: if elizabeth walked in here right now, what single
force could keep me upright, outer circuit of longing, and on this
side of the threshold.

elizabeth absolutely wanted to die, but no one wants to die any way that you can.

it begins with teeth. big beautiful teeth like televisions
stackedup on one another, like the pronouncement
of place:
here we are now.

drones are only the antecedents to themselves except for god. they
are their own futurity, and oriented downward they have none
but ours

in site/
sited.

but *what can* we do
when too many people are standing in our gallery to turn all the
monitors off?!

i ask the visitors, please,
just lower your cameras
while i turn
every monitor off.

well, the morale in this theater is dismal.

how comical the tables seem
after the ghosts have left them
for the monitors.

(please, don't hate the ghosts!)

drones hate ghosts. absolutely.

elizabeth said: ecocide is indicated by fish dying by accident.

elizabeth wanted to look at the east river again.

elizabeth wanted to die today.

elizabeth: is your inner existence just a vacant spin?
elizabeth: mine certainly is not!

elizabeth: even arming the security system each night has its
distinct and mappable pleasures.

2001: the trolley car in the basement needed some repair. we took it out to the courtyard and waited

for the trash from the street and from our everyday lunches to accumulate around it and over it, concealing its damaged parts. one night elizabeth dug it out and asked god if she could lay down and die in it. he said yes. he even cleaned it for her before she climbed in. she told him this was not the way to go; she thought about it again. elizabeth told him she had never done anything like this before in her goddamn life. the trolley had completely fallen apart. it had become a home.

it begins with a theater. and a lot of ideas about how to contend.
i.e. with envy, with this ill-fitting kevlar.

(kevlar should fit;
kevlar is oriented exclusively around a body.)

it begins with a trolley car in the basement and elizabeth in the trash. cleaning out trash, ankle deep in the doorway pushing/ pulling trash across the threshold, out onto the street into long island city.

there's research to be done, elizabeth says and reaches down, picks up a novel.

elizabeth aloud:

'it'll be a real short eon.'

'if we let this door close, another will open.'

elizabeth crosses back over the threshold and closes the door behind her with the trash behind it. she has difficulty finding the stairs that will take her to the basement. god had moved down there already, effectively taking up residence in the broken down trolley car. elizabeth doesn't see him, but suspects that someone is in the basement with her.
presence of.

the trolley has been meticulously cleaned, but gunk falls from the ceiling constantly and lands all over its surfaces, brush it off all you want. it lands on her head, too, and god's. her hair turns white. she selects a seat in the center of the car, sits down, and waits. she can't look up or the gunk'll fall into her eyes. her visual orientation is forward, horizontal toward god, whom she now sees and holds in focus.

elizabeth says she's likely to die there, after all the hard labor she's put in upstairs and into the street. she says, why not? why shouldn't she. what's stopping her. who? god had an easy enough time coming down. a lengthy but vertical(=heterosexual) migration. gravity allied with his angle all the way. elizabeth's tired. she could barely find the stairs through all the trash that was piled up, and now this shit in her hair. bird shit? you could be talking to an angel, elizabeth says. you could be looking at one, now. elizabeth tilts her head back and closes her eyes so she can die. she's never been afraid of death. her fear was never oriented upward, her organization somehow anomalous to the present. elizabeth says, i got all the way here to now without being afraid of the drop or the lookup. elizabeth says i'm a spotter now, too, i suppose. shit keeps falling from the ceiling in the gentle pounding rhythm of trash being put in neat piles on the floor above. elizabeth's eyes won't open now, her lids pressed down on her eyeballs with the weight of two vertical piles, one on each eye. she doesn't move to brush it off because she knows now she's going to die. god's there. she hears the door opening upstairs, shifts in her seat.

it begins in water. and in the air and in the offices of the u.s. american west, winter of. it begins in the air and in the theater of war: the air. it begins with getting up and out of the ocean, trawling trolley cars behind us to collect the floating trash using only our wings.

it begins with hostility, with the optimism of an actor or combatant.

elizabeth says this is the sound of a world with no tomorrow.
elizabeth wants to die today.
she never pressured, but i didn't always *want* to fuck elizabeth when i did. wanting is funny that way.

the best definition of drones is probably the following: "flying, high-resolution video cameras armed with missiles."

i welcome the administration of a different world under a different god. i don't collect suggestions, now. i'm already sick with resolutions.

i am thick with water and kevlar. i am fucking elizabeth in the room i found her in. i am fucking elizabeth in the room i'm tallest in. the room where i remembered getting wet with my imagination, cock nowhere near in hand.

elizabeth: the swimming body does not float or sink.

elizabeth didn't know she was heterosexual the whole damn time.

when i teased her with the soft,
polluted notion
of a vertically oriented fear,
she howled like artillery.

it begins with a boat. in the boat. in a big metal tube. it begins in the pursuit of improved averages in a clattering, fishdead world.

everything oxidizes everything: it begins.
it begins in panavision in technicolor in phase alternating lines/ no color the same.

ahead lies the turning point.

provided there is no longer any human crew aboard, any kind of vehicle or piloted engine can be "dronized."

with elizabeth dead, we circumvented the need for a trolley car. we were flying now. lookedup to. piloted and american.
(winter of)
now,

please, be careful not to drop your cameras
while we turn all the monitors
off.

THEOGONY

elizabeth had long understood living as a process of negation: don't/didn't like.
elizabeth consumed news media without patience; with an astonishing patience for silence.

elizabeth wanted to dig things up with her hands, but did not know where or how to bring that impulse to bear in manhattan or its surrounding boroughs.
elizabeth never grew weary of the subway nor its site specific silences.

elizabeth remained nominally alone, until the annunciation.
elizabeth remained lonely and restless in her solitude.

elizabeth committed herself to science, and then to the museum with its silver, paywalled silence.

this is the story of dark matter. the abortionists of unity, the
doctores angelici; i.e.
a flat multiplicity
of n dimensions, asignifying and
asubjective, i.e., subjunctive.
this is the story designated by indefinite articles, rather than
partitives.

hello, fields of couchgrass! tunnels tunnels
tunnels.
hello, tunnels!
hello, couchgrass! fields and fields of tunnels!

this is the story of the vulgarization of faith
in progress; metonymy substitutes a date
for
traumatic
attacks.

this is the story of light-like behavior.

she beheld the light first as she beheld her hands,
lookeddown upon, illuminated.
elizabeth understood refraction and orientation. she determined
the trajectory of the light source by the angle at which it traveled
from her skin and fingernails to the stairwell's metal railing to her
eye.

the light came from above her, through the ceiling.

what behaved like light was in fact an annunciation, followed by
what behaved like matter, which were angels.

no single thing erupted, cracked, or tilted. elizabeth was at home
in the museum and being pushed apart by what behaved
like light.

she understood it only as behavior first, not provenance or tiding,
and that it was pushing her apart, in opposition to the weaker
force, gravity.

she could not hold, remain integrated, while apprehending.

the angels, who were not matter and could not interact with light
but whose bodies manufacture to the point of emission that which
behaves like light,
saw elizabeth spreading.

each acted to protect her.

it begins with shadow. with a flash of white light, fast-
moving
over distance in every direction such that a source is
indeterminable. it begins with the shadows that form as a result
of the flash and remaining,
are permanent.
the shadows of visiting or proximal structures remain.

elizabeth wasn't afraid.
the threat came from above and vertical fear was then unknown
to her.

it begins with a still. god didn't come up
to meet the angels. with god
below and out of sight, the shock of them was greater.
a force of what behaved like energy concentrated itself. it devoted
itself to elizabeth's dissolution, only preventable
by the angels
themselves.
simultaneously, she felt what could be described as the opposite
of alone. a feeling that behaved like
together.

the feeling that behaved like together—or gravity—could not
withstand the force of dissolution.
only the angels—

'hello.'

with the invention of aviation, the probability for fall increased.
with the invention of aviation, wings became optional rather than
integral.
with the option of
the aspect of
a winged columbia the winged winter with the autumn
underwhelming us the fall that
likely came
the infinite.

it begins in the room they fell into. the room i remember
in the basement in the window mirror window in the burning
fuselage, they fell
and glowed like burning fuselage, behaved like
light like something which behaved like
light, another force, togetherness, a home.

'hi, back.'

the first of the angels to abbreviate the change in elizabeth's
matter was JOAN

JOAN had an infinity of aerial views, i.e. 'good looks'. JOAN was
rocked by the perspectives manifold
before her.
silently, JOAN believed elizabeth was one of them, the angels,
JOAN believed, *i am looking at one, now.*

as elizabeth spread she was silent. the sensation was too
unfamiliar to translate into sound (sound interacts with matter).
she remained unmoved by what behaved like lit
fuselage, that is, what came down at her
by the window, oblique, mirroring down
like sun,
like anvils.

what behaved like matter followed suit: not so much sound
as intestinal fact.

JOAN restored elizabeth's gravity. JOAN provided a sense of
longing outside dissolution, so opposed to loneliness.
JOAN kept upright while the others continued to fall (oh limit).

JOAN knew, 'this is good for us.'
JOAN knew action in the cleanliness
of war.
in "real life"/action
JOAN rocked through infinity
toward elizabeth, the angel,
she presumed.

it begins with a discernment of spirits, with prudence as the
better part of valor.
it begins in the center/conflict; center/state; center/continental
oriented center,
and an annunciation.
it begins with the arrival, and without discernment but with
saints, (k)Catherine, and the angel Michael, for whom *a comfort*
she named and
not a voice.

it begins with aviation, erudition and elan. vertical sovereignty,
mass fish kills, well kills. most
policing is done
from above.

JOAN said: can an aerial view portray
a stable ground?
a moving horse?
all innocence in waging war?

look at that, elizabeth said (silent),
you've made of me a frightened child.

JOAN: what tyranny of *real* activity supplants
inclusion with intrusiveness?
what tyranny;
what tyranny;
not of spacetime as it is, but of an end as we can make it.

JOAN said: fabrication diminishes the dignity of angels—this
is not what we had any right to expect—

JOAN said: oh, this is a death sentence,
unfortunately without the tools you need to properly address the
pain...

JOAN: *un oiseau de peu de creance...*

42

JOAN corrected herself with a beautiful generosity: i remember
only sounds, predominantly that of rending
metal, a local idiom of many
vowels
and grinding consonants, ragged
magnificent vowels, all
vowels, a e i o u urgent, bewildered, and
gigantic.

elizabeth said(silent): obviously, it's too cold to run.
(silent): i love the river because it isn't human and i'm no longer
human

elizabeth remembered(silent): i thought that i was judas, i was
every child in gethsemane.
(silent): outside it's raining, as it always does
in long island city.

JOAN wanted elizabeth to know how much she loved her, and
how her dissolution would be mutually catastrophic. she halted
every force but gravity. she called off all light-like energy and
provided elizabeth with that feeling of
together, risk-free.

elizabeth, aloud, breathless, said: never enough light.

ENLIGHTENMENT

the only way elizabeth could make me come is if i was thinking about other people. not fucking them. just thinking about them.

elizabeth only got off if i came first, inside of her.

this made other people important.

elizabeth was trained as a physicist, thus her intellectual
allegiance remained primarily to forces that behave like energy or
like matter.

elizabeth when asked to explain her infidelity
to linear equations returned with graphs,
warped and discolored by vinegar. she took my hand with one
of hers and traced the running curves and vectors and with the
other hand rubbed my cock.

before the museum, elizabeth worked in a research lab
manufacturing weapons for the us american (winter of) war in
long island city.

when elizabeth met the angel Michael she was thrilled, calledto
tell me she'd successfully discovered vertical desire.

his icon was attractive. he had valor and what she called a "real
cock."

elizabeth told me she didn't want to die and regretted that she
ever had. she thanked god and remembered names of saints she
had forgotten, and others she'd decided to lookup.

elizabeth told me we probably shouldn't see eachother anymore.
she said our mutual attraction pulled her too obliquely across
the scalar plane we'd occupied. she felt loose, flabby. she said her
suicidal ideation had increased. she hated me. she despised me
and was disgusted by our former intimacy to the point of vomiting
involuntarily at the sight of me.

this time when elizabeth arrived at the museum, she recognized
god's position and the threshold of the stairs;
she went straight down.
she took her seat in the body
of the trolley car, broken down, again, lookedup.
the first floor collapsed, first,
then the ceiling above it. the trolley's iron
frame protected her.

from the chasm, the ceiling the floor above, three saints appeared
to elizabeth. she apprehended them despite the
dust, paper,
insulate, and metal that rose
in congress with the falling levels.

the saints had wings and were angels. the saints were Michael,
(k)Catherine and JOAN of arc.

the angel Michael: lie on your back, now.

JOAN: we can help you to identify your fear
and how it's oriented.
we can help you to do that/get your lookup back on track.

(k)Catherine: the requisite shame you feel is normal. i don't love
you, but your usefulness allows me to be intimate, forthcoming,
and accommodating, if not affectionate.

elizabeth (silent): i can't live without affection.

this is the story of finance
digitalizing networks, and intellectual property anxiety.

it begins in the topsoil. depth as the penultimate frontier. it
begins in the fracture, a fractal legal freedom, a disquieted settler
home.

it begins with metal and a funnel and tube. it begins with
potassium chloride to kill the well.

it begins with giant-sized criminals; bad children with electric
fun. it begins with a storm that promised power.

Michael says: prophecy is a dangerous game.
Michael says: you are *feeling* comfort, not *listening* to my voice.

it begins with "EXIT," an exit
but with broader, deeper analytics
of longer-phased nonlinear
reorganizations
of property and
its changing material bases.

this is the story of navigational interface.

elizabeth says (silent): it is so *nice* to be able to focus! to experience (for once) the privilege of value (winter of), of legibility and clarity (winter of).

elizabeth (silent) says:

hi.

the angels say: hi, back.

this is a record of the making of art about "intimacy"
and "exposure." this is surveillance
and the variant conscriptions of power
and of intelligence to each vertical sphere,
having multiplied
from above.

this could be a record of change, its exponents.

saint: pay attention
saint: Pay Attention!

JOAN: fabrication diminishes the dignity of angels.
Michael: she speaks of a comfort, not a voice.
(k)Catherine: lookup, elizabeth!
JOAN: in innocence think only
of waging war.

elizabeth was astonished. she beheld and did not appreciate
the cold that came in through the ceiling deficit that they had
openedup. she wondered if she was christ. she wondered if she
could be christ, or indeed another prophet.
she did not wonder at all. she was rapt with wonder.

it begins without rapture.

with the tubing and solution and the packer. potassium and
intestinal
gases.

willing human, watching war.

it ends with the angel Michael. the unfinished project, the new
generation of nonnative enlightenment.

Michael will not go home.
Michael will rend himself with his statistic, end to end.

Michael will not go home again. he'll identify a lookup toward—in
gratitude—a kinship, maybe, but not
a self.

as is consistent, Michael's renaissance will be violent.

it begins with the long-light hallways, the fifth floors and
mirrored frankenthalers in private,
windowed offices.
did anyone ask after them?

with the target practice
of diplomatic fallout (airmen
being captured); the accelerant of lack
of air-
men; capture; tunnels; sophisticated
measures being
taken.

behold the monitors lit,
again! they hold the desert! hold the burning
fuselage, the brain careening in full
red bloom.

the higher the object, JOAN said, the easier to trace.
JOAN said: never had a firmament burned so brightly and as
steadily
as elizabeth's
own mind.

TRAINING

this is the story of divine intervention.
it begins in the blood, with saints in the blood. it begins with a
hollow shell and annunciation in confidence.
it begins clandestinely—a war machine is/as always
very private.

the angel Michael got on the plane in nevada and got off in new
york city.
Michael was retired.
Michael loved his god, who trafficked in forgiveness, winter of.

Michael entered an impasse
with a proportional relationship with:
nothing; killing.

Michael suffered from face-blindness.
Michael was feral like a dog, had the optical
assimilation of a dog.

Michael, what was your training like?
weeks,
incomplete.

why?

shortages,

workloads/ sequestration.
waivers.

who administered your training?

private
contractors, a few of them.

did you receive a waiver at any time?

yes.

did you receive more than one waiver throughout the course of
your training?

yes.

TEST

1.

(agree/disagree) beyond the hypnosis
of official pacification, there is a war being waged.

how language emerges is rarely a question
of desire (agree/disagree), more often an assertion of collapse-
potential or the reality of being quantified.

there is delight. (agree/disagree).
attribute it to nameless callers, or the wanton dripping
of your cock; the seven brightly glowing generations
of innumerable squid; to you, angelic cup, and you.

(agree/disagree) i feel insurmountable by my exhaustion, i feel
divined by
what was told to me at court
square by
the female god, the wife of god.
i had had no idea of the importance
of wives.

2.

grimace. taste your grimace. be alone with your expression and be
grateful for its privacy.
it's rare.

i am angry and devout. i am circled and unholy, -holy. i am
kneeled before and over
and over again by some providential candidate.

be graceful. feel war and tend to others. observe grace without
opinion and wear it without function.
make it available to all and in all warzones.
worship its organizational qualities.

be just. a field, a field of endlessly tall structures(humans?). i
mean a field of endlessly tall people. keep all of them alive and in
good conscience.

(agree/disagree) war is not invisible, just like capital is not
invisible.
pixelated and constant, who is not waging? wait
'til i tell you :)

know the offices. they are manifold and sensate. they are
universally loved and collectively despised. oh, find me. identify
obedience and make it too ugly to bear. take stock in your own
hideousness.
make forever sounds of exuberance.

(agree/disagree) euphoria behaves with and in unhappiness in
unpredictable ways. it swells and sublimates. it comes again and
again. it loves to be with the faint of heart to show them that their
ugly submission might have merit.
it teaches them "desire."

try harder to understand what i am telling you.

collapse-potential: the volume of forgiveness granted per each individual for the lack of euphoria evinced.

every person has their own, unique statistic.

collapse-potential: how frequently/infrequently an independent editor in new york city has taken kindly to your work and/or appearance.

3.

collapse-potential: your tendency to love people who do not challenge you.

yes, i am lonely. i am outperformed by my regret and tableless in my deceit.
i have forgotten the consequence of screening.

(agree/disagree) you think, they have gotten away from the subject: war.

i apologize for your perceptual failure.

resolution-targets: Resolution Test Targets are used to measure the accuracy or performance of an imaging system for applications such as microscopy or imaging. Resolution Test Targets are inserted into an imaging system to provide measurement capabilities. Resolution Test Targets use a variety of patterns including Ronchi or star to measure a system's resolution. High precision models are also available for demanding or precise measurement requirements.

replace willfullness with personal guide decisions. replace pleasure with the certainty of victory. rebuke the impulses you feel to engage in the discernment of spirits.

believe, truly and on site,
that they are all angels.

(agree/disagree) elizabeth crosses your mind. elizabeth evinces the acuteness of euphoria abandoned. she has exhausted the collective with her capacity to love. she brings herself to climax without stimulation, by will alone.

*(agree/disagree) there is mourning. there are boulevards that flood
with it each june. there are heretics who burn for it each june, july,
and august. there is nothing in the way of it.*

a resolution-target: (agree/disagree) is mapping sight.
*a resolution-target: (agree/disagree) is a cleared expanse; noise in
action; is in the clearing; in the wide, silent commas.*

*resolution-target: (agree/disagree) is commencement; climax; a
painstaking facsimile of pleasure.*

*foundationally, there is mourning. the translation of which is
an essay in silence. the reality of which is unmappable, yet not
invisible.*
it requires (oh, Michael.) *a different imaging system.*

*(agree/disagree) i will not mourn for
elizabeth.*

APOCALYPSE

this is the story of void. it begins
with the abysmal sound of
isolation;

this is the story of baths: it begins with preheated sound-
meal, cartographers' missed
tunnels, phonetic, intimate
translations.

this is the story of drones
in heat.

this is the futureperfect subjunctive.
this is ringing with defunct
potential;
this is *energaia*.

JOAN knew church militant from
church triumphant; she knew the answer to
the call was hot,
hot,
hot.

elizabeth, meanwhile, was shadowed by her guilt, unmoved by
hypocrisy, unmoved by the promise of an orgasm.

Heat death is a theory based on the second law of thermodynamics about how the universe will end. Heat death occurs as the universe moves towards maximum entropy and minimum temperature.

For those who believe in progress, the apocalypse becomes superfluous, since it was only ever necessary as a precondition for the "kingdom."

The kingdom always arrived, because it was always already there. And it was always there because it arrived continually.

In USAmerica, "apocalyptic" and "anti-apocalyptic" are still recognizable in the (beloved) differentiation between "evolutionary" and "revolutionary."

elizabeth waffled with the us american
(winter of)belief that apocalyptic events are
unnecessary.
elizabeth grappled with the indexicality
of an analog photograph in the country of her monitor—a secret
index by which she may refer to
redemption.

seated in the trolley with a vague unease, she sensed the void
stemming from the fact that her body had lost its substance, that
she had been volatilized, stripped of reality, life, voice, the noises
she made when moving about, and had been turned into a mute
image that flickers for a moment on the screen, then vanishes into
silence.

JOAN with weak messianic power disordered elizabeth's
past and present; set aside her temporal questions.

"In fact, matter as a visible object is of no great use any longer...
Give us a few negatives of a thing worth seeing, taken from different
points of view, and that is all we want of it. Pull it down or burn it
up, if you please.
Two is the smallest
unit of Being."

elizabeth was struck by the receptiveness of the trolley car;
its receiving surface suggested that her optical device, her eye, was
also receptive, rather than productive.
through a small aperture in the door to the dark room, JOAN saw
god and elizabeth in the same frame.

Since the viewer had to enter the classical camera obscura in order to see its images, he was also a receiver.

So long as Christianity and Platonism were the dominant forces within Western thought, the notion that light enters the human eye from outside was unproblematic; illumination was, after all, a privileged signifier for both God and the demiurge.

"Every body fills the surrounding air
with infinite images of itself," Leonardo wrote in one notebook entry. "All bodies together, and each by itself, give off to the surrounding air an infinite number of images...
each conveying the nature, color and form of the body which produces it," he observed in another.

This activity is self-presentational, and our look is its "lodestone."

An "unfinished universality" is one oriented to the future.

(splash)
(ow)

JOAN gazed fishily at elizabeth through the aperture, convinced
she was one of them, one of the vertebrate/
invertebrate angels that live scarcely below
street level.

JOAN thought, she's a poem!

the arc of the world, JOAN said, is not a teleology, neither is it
eschatological. apocalypse, she said, is an unnecessary,
underhanded form of singing.

after elizabeth stopped dying, JOAN approached the small river
overwhich the trolley car stooped.
god lookedover, an involuntary human
shield, and drew out laws the dead could
break.

grieving and sick
with it, JOAN reverberated back up
the stairs and through the apertures in concrete echoing
the trolley car and mourning elizabeth dead upon
its skeletal frame.

JOAN made a little diagram. the tenor and the vehicle; the opera
singer and the trolley car; elizabeth in a trolley car in a state of
decomposure.

it's translation, in a way. in/onto a monitor, diagram— 300 little
notes become a playlist. lyrics filter in. we burrow.

the parts that feel important. the heat, the health, the mud, the
dance. the blue mud felt important. every bridge doesn't
connect.
each tunnel.

he is important, god. his obsession with cinema, with burrowing.

we are in visionary
company. modernand
ethical.

it begins with the necessity
of an apocalyptic event being
undermined by a new administration.

it begins with the subjunctive of futures and the radical will, *if*, to be.

this is the story of visionary company. elizabeth and myself,
elizabeth and JOAN, elizabeth and Michael angelus,
elizabeth and G O D.

how many monitors make a museum, an opera house, a movie
theater? how few?
this is the story of the endless proliferation of movie theaters, of
theaters, of action on
all monitors
all present.

it begins on a thursday, which is to say the day prioritized to
memory.

FILM CLIP

vous etes la fille. un oiseau de peu de foi.

CUT

it begins in colored plastic, colored glass, multi-colored mud.
the example of the miracle
of framework.

this is the story that has to be cheap
to shoot
on location in long island city
no travel or
housing costs; illustrating time
is difficult.

it begins with having fun!

it *means* transformation and not death which i don't believe is a
contradiction in terms but a material possibility of conditions.

what's it like to be ugly
and smart?

a hit at a funeral.
CUT

elizabeth's funeral exceeded the time
spent dying.

JOAN wept from the aperture; the procedure of mourning began
in the basement.

the acid. heat. proleptic
effusion. *fuck* (paul)de man. de faraway
places.

once you're in duration you're really in

ou pas

hear that, bird? it's charming
to talk to birds.

these monitors are a
filmmaker's nightmare.

pruning requires simple but precise gestures.
movies can be
harrowing.

a mental landscape
sucks.

god, had he been there, would not have been transparent.

it begins with this exteriority.
the elaborate anti-francophone
conundrum of the selfless; what if,
hear me out, herr benjamin was *incorrect*, translation *can't*
preserve the strange. you are either in or out of duration.

an ending is not destruction; apocalypse is only the first person
subjunctive of revelation.

TRIAL

I cannot answer your first question, because it does not work.

The trial was like JOAN's, but it began a quarter of a century after Elizabeth's death. The defendant was exhausted, but the prosecution was avid. They were prepared and had a quarter century jump. Elizabeth, propped up on her trolley seat, apprehended her accusers, daringly.

I was proud of her, the way she, dead, comported herself in her own defense.
She would not compromise her integrity for immortality.

Elizabeth's indictments read as follows:

"Operating within a disruptive economy;
abandoning a field;
misprizing valued work;
mimicking silence; loving silent places."

Elizabeth wasn't ugly. She looked a lot like me, in life, but a quarter century older. After another quarter of a century, she had eroded to her core. She was buried by the ocean, you see. Long *Island* City.

Rising tides.

Elizabeth had not killed herself, she merely descended the stairs. The angels, despite their best efforts, did the rest.

OFFICIAL TRANSCRIPT OF THE PROCEEDINGS
(JUNE 2026)

TESTIMONY: JOAN
    SHE COULD HAVE BEEN ONE OF US. SHE COULD HAVE BEEN AN ANGEL. I COULD HAVE SAID, GODDAMN IT THAT'S ONE OF US!
    SHE HAD A WHOLENESS LIKE YOU COULDN'T BELIEVE. LIKE A COLUMN OR AN ATOM. AND WE SPLIT HER. LIKE ARTILLERY OR FISSION. WE COULDN'T HELP IT. I TOLD HER.
    WE TRIED TO INTERVENE. SHE SPOKE TO US. SHE ACTUALLY SPOKE AND WE HEARD HER. TELEPATHICALLY SHE TOLD US WHAT SHE COULD NOT LIVE WITHOUT.
    SHE WAS INDEFENSIBLE. I GUESS I MEAN WE COULDN'T DEFEND HER. WE WATCHED HER DISSOLUTION AND SHE FELT OUR EBULLIENCE.
    SHE MUST BE EXHAUSTED. I AM SO SORRY, ELIZABETH.

Elizabeth didn't hear her. The trial was a joke. Elizabeth was ugly and exhausted. There was nothing that she could have done to defend herself. The angels, saving JOAN, were absent—and JOAN was unreliable.

Elizabeth was stuffed with something similar to corn-meal, something ground.

A preservative measure is a violent intrusion.

Meal spread from her into the small basement river, clotting.

A trial must begin with proof, i.e., the ability to prove your own
god, to pinpoint a caesura in a stream of exits. Pink, streaming
bereavement, i.e., negative evidence
proves the god and your arrival through the same door.

Stairs represent something for Elizabeth. She feels an inclination to follow; all stairs descend.

When Elizabeth raises posthumous objections to the art, it's noise she's talking about. Which is to say: the indictment of revelation by the proliferation of false revelation.

Elizabeth was dry, a cadaver leaking dust; there was a broom and dust pan; they were not just props.

Elizabeth was offered something that resembled a catechism.

It began with a synod with props.
It began with the clerical props that give credence to a verdict; innocent or guilty.

There was no indication of any measures having been taken for the defendant's security.
JOAN flailed in indignance; her protests bored the prosecutors, appalled the judge.

EXHIBITS:
Corn meal
Broom
Dustpan
Camera (left)
Camera (right)
Camera (back office)
Camera (service entrance)
Camera (elevator)
Satellite (1-3)
Wigs
Wings
Pews
Bone
Trolley car
River
Door (1-2)
Monitor (1-??)
APPEARANCES:
Louise
Saint JOAN

The judge was remote; he presided via monitor. Within the
courtroom, he could neither be seen nor heard. His verdict would
be delivered via satellite.

The jury was impartial and in motion. They streamed constantly
through the door.
They apprehended walls of monitors that waited, silently, to
flicker on,
again.

The river in part caught, the thick walls and doors
irradiated witness. Jury stirring,
hung down one by one to see.

Elizabeth found it hard to get their attention, or differentiate
between them.

Soon, meal was spreading all over the floor.

LOUISE:
    i met elizabeth at the museum. she wasn't out, but she gave me reason to believe she was interested, at least. i found her irresistible. i liked that she'd had training and had abandoned her field. i liked that she hated the art at the museum. she often devalued my work, or interrupted my visual field. she wanted everything quiet where it couldn't be. she wanted me to tell her she was beautiful in a way that she could feel desired but not threatened. that's not rare; i get that a lot; femme energy, femme woe, whatever you want to call it. she liked it enough to encourage it.

    elizabeth was straight so she didn't identify as a bottom, but she bottomed. she loved it. she was opposed to overt expressions of pleasure. what i'm trying to say is that she was quiet, efficient. i dont know how, but she made me quiet, too.

    i was in love with elizabeth, but she was straight. she was in love with Michael, who was a killer.

DEFENSE:
    Aren't all men murderers?

LOUISE:
    yes.

PROSECUTION:
    Leading the witness.

THE COURT:
    [SILENCE]

LOUISE:
    when god moved into the basement—of the museum, that is—everything changed. she felt...descendant, elizabeth did. i don't know how to describe it. she let me go, and i guess things started piling up.

100

DEFENSE:
   Exhibit A. [Defense brings out BROOM and DUSTPAN]

LOUISE:
   *use that to clean her up. use that to clean all this up now.
want me to do it? i'm working with the defense; i'll clean her up.
people used to say we looked alike, that she looked like my older
sister. i have an older sister, and she isn't elizabeth. i don't know. i
know we didn't last long, but she stayed with me, you know? some
people stay with you.*

JOAN was exquisitely lonesome after Elizabeth died. She had loved Elizabeth, or at least an idea of Elizabeth.

JOAN kept trying to find a picture.

To hate the feast of eagles; in secret, secret one and another bird appear.

INTERLUDE: CIRCLES

it begins with the trepidation of spheres, halo to halo.

by way of brief summary:
each planet (sun moon earth) had its halo
possessedof its distinct vibrations
and frequencies according to
numerical ratios that created a harmony
in their movement, though not audible to humans.

though imperceptible to men (most men), its subtle harmony
rocked the planet and improved its collective quality of life.

"In around 1294, Dante writes *La Vita Nuova*, depicting Love as an angel who appears to the poet and declares, 'I am as the center of a circle, to which all parts of the circumference stand in equal relation, you however, are not so.'

Of this quote, scholar John Freccerro writes, 'For Dante, as for most thinkers of his time, the spatial and temporal perfection represented by the circle precluded its use as a symbol for anything human.' The perfect sphere associated with Dante's version of Paradise and angel of love was something that had to be earned by duration through hell, and could not be naturally reconciled with the inherent deficiency of the human soul. The distance between perfection and humanity was to these 13th century Italian philosophers and thinkers, insurmountable.

Fast forward to 1580. Poet John Donne is 8 years old and Francis Drake, under the auspices of Elizabeth I, returns from his trip around the globe, becoming the first Englishman to accomplish this feat. Donne himself would travel greatly, embarking on several dubious, state-sponsored campaigns in Spain and writing extensively about it. Integral to these endeavors is the map-making technology of the compass, a precise and attractive tool that allows the user to draw a near perfect circle by delineating a complete area of equal distance from its center (the center being presumably Europe or England). As a coterie poet of the Elizabethan court, whose coterie included not just friends, but acquaintances from whom he was attempting to extract money, it makes sense that Donne includes such imagery. The tools involved with mapmaking are often depicted on illuminated maps, atlases, and travel writings, highlighting the human hand as integral to the shaping of the world. Deploying such imagery in his poems paints Donne as a poet worthy of his imperial moment.

To get from Dante's angel to the 'stiff twin compasses' of the 'Valediction,' the circle had to undergo an ideological/semiotic rebrand. From the transcendent and angelic to the secular and intellectual, a metamorphosis from the glyph of the divine to that of the immortal human soul, to a basic tool for rendering the known world as a manageably conquerable shape.

Donne's poem, 'Valediction,' however, refuses to walk any lines between the profane and the divine, the scientific and the beatific. Donne collapses these categories into a single one: the human. Freccerro asserts, 'his [Donne's] most famous image, that of the compass, protests, precisely in the name of incarnation, against the neo-Petrarchan and neoplatonic dehumanization of love. It makes substantially the same point made by Love to the young Dante three hundred years before: angelic love is a perfect circle, while beasts move directly and insatiably to the center...' Donne would conclude that man, especially this man, is no beast, and is redeemed not by Christ but by Love.

Donne's compass of Love, so to speak, represents thus not just an image but an active process, the drawing of the circle, the maintenance of perfect boundaries that human love, done right, can achieve. Undoing and reworking those centuries of Italian thought and poetic imagery, Donne puts the soul back in the human body, but retains its immortality, holiness and faculty for perfection. (For a more Copernican analysis of Donne, see commentary on *Good Friday, 1613 Riding Westward*)"

HUNGER

let's not get sick.
elizabeth said.

abstract
disease into
color.

it begins with red
for anger.

blue, the precise
material ways
poetry is a force
against effacement.

blue hunger. blond eyes.

it begins
to shade that green theme.

this is the story of self-digestion, which is to say:
hunger.

(there's a big difference between autophagia and cannibalism,
elizabeth said)

this is the story of the premier celebrity resident
of heaven: JOAN,
whose riskof effacement was to claim self-coincidence to perform
the talk of recognition in time.

for what?
a calculated risk, which is to say a poem, the transforming life
of eructation, i mean, surfacehunger,
i mean skin.

in the transforming life of language, the skin is
hegel and his night his night his night is now now

now.

it begins with what we find/ her in an embryo, elizabeth
elizabeth taking down the stairs herself, elizabethan heat, in self-
concious ontologies of
tragedy; in gargoyle, i mean garbage, topped;
heaped arrangements of
electric vehicles.

elizabeth, necrotic, won the day!!
JOAN, her misguided advocate, was diligent in her transcription
of the silent
testimony.

Arcadia, reoccupied
again.

this is the story defined by holes, hole-making.

bored with the proleptic, elizabeth moved on to the protoplasmic,
the hungry the communally corruptible. lookingup, she saw
things that could not be disproven; watcher by watched.
lookingup to have her photograph taken, again, by the UAV above
L I C, the museum a frequent target, elizabeth continued with her
broom. she gave up. inside, she took up one of many filled black
plastic bags and took the stairs down into the basement, heaving
the heavy garbage bag before her. the spectral trolley car was
shaking in dustlight. the UAV hovered solely outside the door.

JOAN, invisible to elizabeth
was capable of strong emissions of interference but
thick walls of concrete subdued them.

not-this, elizabeth slipped and caught herself on the third stair.
god held his breath.
it wasn't night but it was close, and now elizabeth's descent
slipped into certainty. no return, spectral or otherwise.

this could be a poem, she said. i could be a goddamn poet
of the night
and now, she murmured. JOAN was rapt:
she's one of us. i am looking at one *now*.

it begins with a righteous syllabus, an incorruptible document,
the story of heartburn, which is to say
self-maintenance.

if there was something to begin it would be hunger.
the lookup, JOAN said, is the digestion of the green theme of your
own end.
we could be absolutely ferreted
out and still
not know to run
the interference of which
we are
fully capable.

this is the content of sense-experience. it begins in the dark under
the laboratory
boot,
so to speak, which is to say,
the exscription of contemporary
poetry.

this is animal disappointment.

de anima taste and seeing
be forms of touch.

NOSTALGIA

i spoke of

nostalgia as a tense
that begs
for a present that prioritizes
the future
perfect; i.e.

i spoke of
comfort not

a voice.

i said,
there were eggs in the water, the small river where elizabeth
looked down to greet them, bobbing up
and down; they were excitable, violable, envious little
eggs.

she said, lucky we are not born
in the boring
century   world made of worlds.

left by the fixers not the angels, elizabeth could hold them,
the eggs, in her hands.

elizabeth had turned something off, inside, and let the eggs
represent for her that thing which she neither neglected nor
wished for.

the first nostalgia
the angels did say:

ova in excelsis
deo!

this is the beginning
of an endless series of referents. the ivan hoes and most
importantly

the whales.
the tell tale exhaustion of a zealous year, the seep under
the big green door.

elizabeth was perfectly aware of her hypocrisy; her material
conditions were what needed change.

without comment, elizabeth descended the stairs.
all ulterior and anterior motive
lost, all corruption blithely
disentangled, she descended unto the
trolley-god world.

decisiveness abandoned, elizabeth had a *fine* time
finding her footing
on the stairs.

this is the story of dark. it begins in the stairwell, shielded
from view, from the electric light that hummed
out of the monitors,
soft into the galleries
and the lobby.

before anybody dies, there is all this pleasure.

this is the story of we
the featherless, the undergirded
propeller, the finger
and attachments.

this is a combination of being ripped
to shreds and happening to find
pleasure in disorientation and
the drift.

this is the story of deployment and counter-
return.

this is the misspelling of terror
terroir;
error;
elizabeth.

it begins with a new trial.
with proving your own god
in the sawdust, in the corn-
meal.

it begins with alphanumeric
questions of responsibility; it begins with elizabeth's accountant,
hereon referred to as JOAN; it begins with a record
that accounts for a more recent trial.

it begins with a protest
riot
rampage
runner
terror
lookup
elizabeth wrote
down each word above in its own heat and
weight and translated each into another.

it begins with the
mycelial refusals
without which we could not
get along,
who regulate
the speed
of this air.

i said, what if i looked at you, elizabeth,
and said
translation is this *capitalist* thing,
or something just
like that,
and we gave up on everything you loved?

elizabeth said, what i loved was the resurrection
of dead languages, which i suppose
is the translation of capital in its own
right. (winter of)/
(failure to).

this is the story of age and elizabeth
aged.

and a poem is a limit,
is a river, or is
clots of human-
meal, is
orderwords and mirror
words,
otherwords. (oh,
limit)

this is the story of we
at the winter of
aged out and
haloed hello
to angels.

hi back.

Acknowledgments:

A version of MUSEUM was published as "here i am now" in *A) GLIMPSE)OF), The Eccentric Issue.* Spring 2019.

Notes:
The transcript on page 8 is from the transcript of a US drone attack on February 21, 2010 obtained by the *LA Times* through a Freedom of Information Act request.
http://documents.latimes.com/transcript-of-drone-attack/

The quotations on page 109 are from the following article: Freccero, John. "Donne's "Valediction: Forbidding Mourning"." ELH 30, no. 4 (1963): 335-76. Accessed February 28, 2021. doi:10.2307/2871909.

Language on page 78 is adapted from *Endzeit und Zeitende (End-Times and the End of Time, 1959)* by Günther Anders. Translated from the German by Hunter Bolin. Excerpted and republished by *e-flux Journal* #97 - February 2019. https://www.e-flux.com/journal/97/251199/apocalypse-without-kingdom/

Language on page 80 is adapted from Kaja Silverman's *The Miracle of Analogy: or The History of Photography, Part 1* (Stanford University Press, 2015) p. 17.

The "mycelial refusals" on page 131 belong to Jeff Voss.

My sincere thanks to the editors of the Propeller Books Contemporary Poetry series, Lucas Bernhardt and Jan Verberkmoes, as well as Dan DeWeese for the design. My deepest gratitude to my friends and family who made this book possible: Jeff Voss, Emma Wippermann, Sophie Seita, Ian Anderson, Mollie Bernstein, Ulrich Jesse K Baer, my sister, Torey Akers, and my parents Stephen and Gertrude Akers.

Louise Akers is a poet living in Brooklyn, New York. They earned their MFA from Brown University in May of 2018, and received the Keith and Rosmarie Waldrop Prize for Innovative Writing in 2017 and the Confrontation Poetry Prize in 2019. Their chapbook, *Alien Year*, was selected by Brandon Shimoda for the 2020 Oversound Chapbook Prize.

IN THE PROPELLER BOOKS CONTEMPORARY POETRY SERIES

Kirsten Ihns, *sundaey*

Abraham Smith, *Dear Weirdo*

Louise Akers, *Elizabeth/The Story of Drone*